RUNNING AWAY

Compiled by Pat Edwards and Wendy Body

Acknowledgements

We are grateful to the following for permission to reproduce copyright material: Associated Book Publishers (UK) Ltd for an extract from *Shining Rivers* by Ruth Dallas (Methuen Children's Books); Jonathan Cape Ltd on behalf of the Estate of Liam O'Flaherty for the story 'His First Flight' from *The Short Stories of Liam O'Flaherty*; the author's agents for the poem 'What Has Happened to Lulu?' from *Collected Poems of Charles Causley* (pub Macmillan); William Collins Sons & Co Ltd for an extract from *David Copperfield* by Charles Dickens, simplified by Norman Wymer (pub Collins ELT); The Hamlyn Publishing Group for the story 'A Narrow Escape' from *The Modern Children's Library of Knowledge Book 7* by Felix Salten; William Heinemann Ltd for the poem 'Meeting' from *Taxis and Toadstools* by Rachel Field (Worlds Work Ltd, Windmill Press); Scholastic Inc for an extract from *Princess and Minerva* by Carolyn Lane. Copyright © 1982 by Carolyn Lane; Franklin Watts, Inc for an extract from *Mayday! Mayday!* by Hilary Milton. Copyright © 1979 by Hilary Milton. Used with permission of the publisher, Franklin Watts, Inc. Pages 38-9 were written by Bill Boyle.

We are grateful to the following for permission to reproduce photographs: ARDEA, pages 88-9 (A & E Bomford), 88 inset (P Morris), 89 inset (B L Sage); COO-EE Picture Library, page 95; Columbia Pictures Industries Incorporated, page 39; National Portrait Gallery, page 38.

Illustrators, other than those acknowledged with each story, include Peter Foster pp.16-7; Dave Bowyer pp.38-9; Jenny Beck p.41; Jean Cooper-Brown pp.44-5; David Bone pp.58-9; John Ward pp.60-5 and p.76; Gill Elsbury pp.74-5.

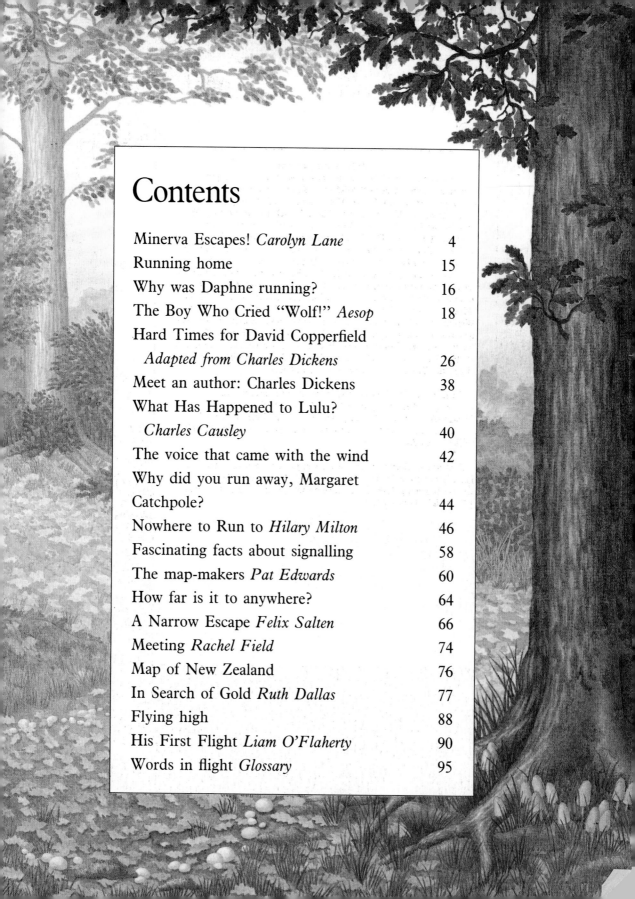

Contents

Minerva Escapes!

Minerva is not the sort of cat who likes being inside things. Even when she's at home she likes to come and go as she pleases.

But she's not at home now! Two weeks ago, in a moment's forgetfulness on a moonlight mouse chase, she dashed out in front of a car. Strangers brought her to the vet who fixed her broken leg. But no one came to claim her . . . until dear old Mrs Weatherington. She thinks Minerva looks just like her poor dead Callie and hopes she might be as cuddlesome and affectionate as Callie was. But not Minerva!

All the way to Mrs Weatherington's home Minerva yowled, scratching at the sides of the case and racketing furiously around. From the front seat, Mrs Weatherington's voice, chattering at her all the way, sounded strained and nervous, and once in a while Minerva felt the car wildly swerving from side to side.

Grateful as she was to the old lady, Minerva was determined to make a run for it the very moment the lid was raised, and when the car finally came to a jolting halt, she gathered herself into a crouch at the bottom of the case, ready to spring. Through the open door of the car, a warm, beautiful summer breeze drifted past the holes in her carrying case — the first whiff of the outdoors she'd had in *weeks* — and Minerva was wild to be free.

But to her dismay, she felt the case being hauled out of the car, then carried up a flight of steps, then set abruptly down — with the lid still firmly closed! There was the sound of a key in a lock, a door squeaked open, and then she was suddenly lifted up once more, then plunked down again. Two loud bangs told her that the door — and then another door — had been closed behind her.

"There you are, Kitty. We're home, safe and sound. You may come out now."

Suddenly there was dazzling sunshine all around — and with a loud, joyful meow, Minerva leaped over the edge of the carrying case and up to the highest, airiest place she could find. Pots of geraniums lined the sill of the newly opened window, but Minerva squeezed herself among them, pressing her nose to the screen. The light summer breeze washed delightfully over her, and the sun she had not seen in so many long, dark days warmed her fur. Outside there were tall trees, and a wide lawn of uncut grass. This was going to be a fine place to stay — at least long enough to get back enough strength for a journey home — and at once Minerva meowed to be let out.

"Oh, no, no, no, Kitty. You may sit on the windowsill any time you choose, but you may not go out. I have never believed that pets should be allowed to roam about outdoors. My Callie went out only when I took her on a leash — and, oh, how she did enjoy a nice walk around the block. You just settle down now, Kitty, and maybe in a day or two, when you're used to things, I'll unpack Callie's old leash and collar, and you and I can go for a walk together. Won't that be fun? In the meantime, I'm just going to keep you here in the kitchen. Be a good kitty, now, and I'll fix you up a nice litter box."

All at once Minerva was alone, pushing helplessly at the screen, yearning for the feel of the green grass against her fur, the roughness of the tree trunks beneath her weakened claws. Leaping from the windowsill, she paced the tiny kitchen, moving from one corner to another, looking for another way out. But the back door was firmly shut, and so was the door that led from the kitchen into the rest of the house. There was no way out at all!

Jumping back to the windowsill and cramming herself uncomfortably in among the geraniums, Minerva suddenly realized that somehow she had exchanged one cage for another!

When Mrs Weatherington came back — hastily slamming the door behind her — she brought with her not only a litter box, but a huge wicker basket with a plump mattress in it.

"Just see what I've brought for you" she said, setting it underneath the kitchen table. "It's Callie's old bed. Won't that be a fine place to sleep? Come try it, Kitty!"

But Minerva had no intention of trying out Callie's old bed. She wanted to sleep *outdoors*, not in any silly wicker basket, and she would just stay on the windowsill until Mrs Weatherington understood. Firmly bunching herself up into a ball, Minerva sat motionless, glaring. Even the saucer of milk that suddenly appeared on the floor just below the windowsill did not bring her down, and it was plain to Minerva that Mrs Weatherington — fluttery and upset — hadn't the faintest idea what to do about her.

"You're not like my Callie at all," she kept saying sadly, "even though you do look like her. Callie was so cuddlesome and affectionate, and she always came when I called her. I don't understand you, Kitty, I really don't. I should think you'd be glad to have such a good home!"

For a moment Minerva considered coming down and being nice to Mrs Weatherington. The poor lady was trying so hard to please her — and after all, this bright, sunny kitchen was a far better place to be than the dark old cage that had been her home for the past few weeks. Perhaps, when Mrs Weatherington got to know her better, she'd stop mourning for old Callie, and understand that Minerva was an entirely different sort of cat — an independent cat with a need to come and go as she chose.

Though she knew that she was never in this world going to be "cuddlesome and affectionate" like Callie, Minerva could be a perfectly respectable housecat when she wanted to be — and suddenly she wanted to be. A day or two of rest and nourishment, she thought sensibly, would be just the thing to put some meat on her bones, build up her flabby muscles. It was, after all, going to be a long walk home.

It was the sound of the electric can opener — and then the delicious smell of Tastee Tidbits in the air — that finally brought Minerva down, determined to be as decent a housecat as she could manage. Taking the time to rub gratefully up against Mrs Weatherington's ankle, she dived at once into the best and biggest meal she'd had in weeks.

From the start, Mrs Weatherington was good to her. Within a day, Minerva was allowed out of the kitchen, allowed to prowl about the rest of the house wherever and whenever she wished. She could sleep on any piece of furniture that happened to take her fancy, she was welcome in every room — and Mrs Weatherington even moved all the geraniums to the kitchen table so that Minerva could stretch herself full length on the windowsill.

The food was marvellous. Though Minerva would have been more than satisfied with plain old canned cat food, and maybe a saucer of milk now and then, Mrs Weatherington insisted on *cooking* for her, producing such unheard of delicacies as salmon with buttered bread crumbs, warm, frothy mixtures of egg and milk, and nicely broiled fresh mackerel.

In return for all this, Minerva purred frequently, rubbed up against Mrs Weatherington's ankles before and after every meal, even jumped up into her lap on an occasional evening. She was, she thought, a truly model housecat — until the day Mrs Weatherington came hopefully at her with Callie's old collar and leash.

"How about a nice little walk?" she suggested brightly. "I'll just fasten this collar around your —"

In a flash, Minerva had skittered under the sofa and backed herself against the wall. Never in all her independent life had she worn a scratchy collar around her neck — and the thought of parading about at the end of a leash was too ridiculous even to consider. No collar for old Minerva, and no leash either! More than anything, she wanted to be outdoors again — but she was *not* going to be tugged about like a silly, prancing poodle!

Within minutes, Mrs Weatherington had put away the collar and leash, sorrowfully shaking her head and reminiscing about all those lovely walks she'd had with old Callie.

Hopefully, Minerva came out from under the sofa, then scampered to the front door, meowing a pleading "meow!". But Mrs Weatherington, not understanding, was upon her at once, swooping her abruptly up into her arms, carrying her into the kitchen.

"There," she said, plunking Minerva into the litter box beside the back door, "there you are, Kitty. Is that what you want?".

No! Leaping out of the box and over the kitchen table to the windowsill, Minerva clawed wildly at the screen, telling Mrs Weatherington that she'd had enough of boxes, that all she wanted was to be *out*! She wanted to walk on the green grass, to sharpen her claws on a tree trunk — not that silly, falling-over scratching post Mrs Weatherington had provided for Callie — to roll deliciously about, scratching her back, in the stony driveway. She might well come back for supper — yes, she probably would — but in the meantime, she wanted to be *free*!

"You might as well stop that scratching, Kitty," scolded Mrs Weatherington. "You're only ruining the screen — and you know full well that no cat of mine is going to run about outdoors. Now just come down from there, and I'll give you a brand new catnip mouse to play with. And then — you know what? I'm going to think of a nice name for you. It's high time you had a name of your very own."

But Minerva did not want a brand new catnip mouse, nor did she want any name other than the one she already had, given to her by a long-forgotten family, way back when she'd been a tiny kitten — Minerva. As a matter of fact, plain old "Kitty" suited her just fine. Like "Puss", it was a name for a cat that didn't belong to anyone, and despite all the lounging around she'd done in the past few weeks, Minerva knew full well that she was never going to belong to Mrs Weatherington — or anybody else.

Mrs Weatherington didn't know it, though, and as the days went by, she seemed to feel that Minerva was settling down nicely. She no longer clawed at the window screens (no point in risking a broken claw, Minerva felt, if it wasn't going to get her anywhere), nor did she meow forlornly at the front or back door. All *that* ever brought was the immediate sight of that awful collar and leash, dangling from Mrs Weatherington's hand, and the eager suggestion that she put it on now and "come for a walk, like a good kitty".

There was nothing to do, Minerva decided, but to behave like a proper housecat — and keep herself alert at all times for a possible means of escape.

Minerva behaved herself so well that sometimes Mrs Weatherington was a bit careless about keeping doors shut. Once, on a morning when she stood chatting with the milkman, Minerva actually managed to slip out — but before she was halfway down the walk, Mrs Weatherington had snatched her up, hanging firmly on to her until the milkman was gone and the door shut behind him.

"Bad girl!" she scolded Minerva. "Bad, bad Kitty. You know I don't allow you to go prowling about the neighbourhood. Now you just stay inside, where you belong."

Mrs Weatherington immediately became more watchful, and it was a long, long time before another door stood ajar for even a second. This time it happened at night, when a neighbour came to the front door to return something she had borrowed from Mrs Weatherington. To Minerva's delight, the neighbour had no time to stop for a visit, and so the two stood talking in the open doorway. Perfect! If she could just manage to streak out fast enough, thought Minerva, excitedly lashing her tail, she could lose herself in the darkness in no time!

Swiftly, leaping down from the living room windowsill where she'd been enjoying the cool night air, Minerva made a dash for the doorway, zipped through it, and was careening wildly about the dark front yard before Mrs Weatherington could do more than make a useless grab for Minerva's disappearing tail.

"Come back, Kitty, come back, come back!"

But Minerva had no intention of coming back — ever. Fond as she was of Mrs Weatherington, she knew that the tiny, closed-up house she lived in was definitely not the place for old, independent Minerva. The place for Minerva was out here in the cool darkness, out here where there were no walls, and only the wide, starry sky for a ceiling.

Diving through a hedge into the next yard, Minerva did not stop to enjoy the feeling of the fresh breeze ruffling her fur, did not stop to sniff the delicious damp grass, to glance even briefly at the great open sky overhead. For as long as she heard Mrs Weatherington's frantic voice calling into the darkness, Minerva kept on running. She gave no thought to direction, only to the incredible thought that she was *free* — really free!

When the voice finally faded away, Minerva slowed down to as brisk a walk as she could manage with her still gimpy leg. Her sides were heaving, her tongue lolling from her mouth, and she realized that she was far from fit. All those weeks of doing nothing but eating and sleeping had made her muscles go slack, and Minerva knew at once that she'd need a night's rest before she could begin the journey home.

Carolyn Lane   Illustrated by Judith Selleck

13

Running home

Both dogs and cats are well known for their ability to find their way home when lost. Some special sense seems to tell them exactly the right direction to take. Here are two examples of faithful dogs that managed to find their owners after becoming lost.

The Guinness Book of Records tells us of one doggy trek back in the year of 1923. A collie dog named Bobby became lost while his owners were on holiday in the state of Indiana in the United States. The family were sure they would never see their pet again, but six months later, guess who turned up back home in the state of Oregon? Bobby had travelled 3200 kilometres in order to get back to his owners; he had even crossed the Rocky Mountains in the middle of winter.

In October 1973 Whisky, an eight-year-old terrier, proved himself to be a champion traveller. He got separated from his master, a lorry driver, at Hayes Creek — a little place north of Darwin in Australia. Eight months later he found his owner. He had travelled 2720 kilometres across central Australia to be reunited with his owner.

WHY WAS DAPHNE RUNNING?

First question — Who was Daphne?

Daphne was another of the heroines found in the Greek myths. She was the daughter of Peneus, the river god. Daphne wanted to spend her days hunting; she loved the freedom of the forest. She refused to look at any of the young men her father found for her.

But one day, deep in the forest, she met the god Apollo. He was the god of music, poetry and archery and he could also foresee the future. Daphne ran away from him. Apollo was handsome and strong and he wasn't used to girls running away from him.

"Stop!" he cried. "Don't run away. I'm no common shepherd or hunter. I'm the god Apollo and I don't mean to harm you." Daphne had no intention of stopping. She knew all about the Gods and how unfaithful and cruel they could be. She ran even faster. Apollo ran after her and it seemed that he would not catch her, because Daphne was swift and strong. But no one could outrun Apollo. Slowly he gained on her. He had only to reach out his hand and he would touch her. Just at that moment the trees seemed to open and Daphne saw her father's river in front of her.

16

"Help me, Father, save me!"
she screamed.

At that moment the girl was
magically changed into a tree —
a laurel tree. Saddened by what
had happened, Apollo vowed that
from that moment on, this would
be his special tree and all those
people who won in games (or in
war) should wear a crown of
laurel leaves.

Why do we remember these stories?

There is a sweet-scented flowering shrub called "Daphne".
That's the name the Greeks used for the type of laurel tree
found in the Mediterranean area. It was named after
Daphne, daughter of the river god.

Bay leaves, which are often used in cooking, are the
leaves of the laurel tree.

Because of the old story, we see the laurel as a symbol of
victory and peace, and people often speak of looking to your
laurels, which means keeping up a high standard. Another
saying is, "Don't rest on your laurels", which means don't
be satisfied with one success — keep trying. If anyone ever
says it to you, you'll know where it comes from.

THE BOY WHO CRIED 'WOLF!'

An Aesop fable adapted by **PAT EDWARDS**, illustrated by **PETER FOSTER.**

Once there was a shepherd boy who longed for adventure.

What a boring job this is, watching silly sheep!

19

But of course, all was peaceful up in the meadows.

So the villagers went back to their work.

And the shepherd boy spent the rest of the day laughing.

Two days later, the same wicked thought popped back into the boy's mind. Off to the village he raced again.

Up the hill raced the villagers.

And once again all was peaceful and still.

This time some of the villagers grumbled on their way back home.

The shepherd boy waited a whole week before he played the trick again.

The villagers were not sure whether to believe him but he was very convincing.

Up the hill they raced behind the boy!

And down they came again, angry and disgruntled.

The shepherd boy realised he couldn't go on tricking the villagers.

What a pity I have to stop. Now it's dull and boring again.

But that very day...

BAA!

BAA!

BAA!

The boy was terrified.

A wolf – a real wolf! Oh, what will I **do**?

BAA!

BAA!

BAA!

BAA!

24

The wolf was big and fierce. The boy needed help from the villagers.

Wolf! Wolf! Help! A Wolf is eating my sheep!

But this time no one believed him.

Hard times for David Copperfield

David Copperfield, by Charles Dickens, is a very famous book. It tells the life-story of an English boy about 160 years ago.

David's father died before he was born. Several years later, his mother married again, to a Mr Murdstone. David never liked his new step-father (or Mr Murdstone's sister, either). Once when Mr Murdstone beat David, David bit him on the hand!

Shortly after this, David was sent to boarding school and his life became utter misery. Mr Creakle was a headmaster who enjoyed beating boys, and he especially enjoyed beating David. At last holiday-time arrives and David goes home — home to his beloved mother, his dear nurse Peggotty . . . and the Murdstones.

When I returned home, I felt like a stranger. I walked towards the house, looking at the windows. I wondered if Mr Murdstone or his sister were watching me.

As I entered the house, I heard my mother quietly singing. I went softly into the sitting-room and spoke to her.

"Davy! My dear boy!" she cried. She came across the room and kissed me, again and again.

Peggotty ran into the room and danced with happiness.

Mr Murdstone and his sister were out. This was better luck than I hoped for.

We had dinner together — my mother, Peggotty and I. Afterwards we sat by the fire and talked. I told them about my unhappy life at school, and they were very sorry for me.

I suddenly remembered what Mr Barkis said to me that morning when I left home for boarding school. He took me on his horse and cart to catch the London coach and I remembered sitting up beside him and what he had said to me. "Oh, Peggotty! Mr Barkis wants to marry you," I told her.

Peggotty threw up her hands and laughed. "The man wants to marry *me!*" she cried.

My mother looked worried. I noticed a great change in my mother. Her face was still very pretty, but she looked tired and ill.

"You won't marry him, Peggotty, will you? Not yet!" said my mother. "Don't leave me! I can't manage without you."

"I'll never leave you, my dear," Peggotty promised. She comforted my mother like a child.

At ten o'clock we heard the sound of wheels.

"It's late!" my mother said with fear in her voice. "David, go to bed — quickly!"

When I saw Mr Murdstone in the morning, at breakfast, I felt uncomfortable. It was our first meeting since I bit his hand. Mr Murdstone looked at me but said nothing.

Miss Murdstone gave me a dark look. "Oh, you have come back!" she said. "How long are the holidays?"

"A month, ma'am."

"They began yesterday. So one day has gone," she returned.

Miss Murdstone marked off in a little note-book each day as it passed.

The holidays gave me no greater happiness than they gave Miss Murdstone. Nobody seemed to want me — except Peggotty. In the evenings, I sometimes escaped and sat with Peggotty in the kitchen. I was happy with her.

One evening when I was leaving the sitting-room, Mr Murdstone stopped me. "I see that you like servants better than us!" he said. "I am not pleased. You will spend no more time with that servant, Peggotty. That is an order!"

Every evening afterwards I sat in the room in silence, waiting for bedtime.

I was not sorry when the holidays ended and I went back to school.

I remember nothing that happened at school till my birthday. After breakfast on that day a teacher came to the schoolroom and said: "David Copperfield is wanted".

I brightened. "Peggotty has sent me some cakes for my birthday," I thought. I hurried to Mr Creakle's room.

Mr Creakle was eating his breakfast, with his stick beside him. Mrs Creakle was holding a letter in her hand.

Mrs Creakle gave me a chair and sat beside me. "David," she said gently, "I have heard some very sad news — about your mother. Your mama has been very ill. This morning I received a letter telling me that she — She is dead."

I cried and cried. I cried till I could cry no more. No child ever felt a mother's death so deeply.

I returned home next day. Peggotty ran out of the house and took me in her arms. We both broke down.

I went into the sitting-room. Mr Murdstone and his sister took no notice of me. They said not one kind word.

I watched my mother laid to rest beside my father. As I left the church, I looked sadly at our house. It was still so pretty, but the love and happiness were gone. Miss Murdstone now sent Peggotty away. With a sad heart, I said 'good-bye' to my dear nurse.

"I won't go far away. We'll still see each other," Peggotty promised me.

She stayed with her brother at Yarmouth — and two weeks later she married Mr Barkis.

I was very lonely without Peggotty. Mr Murdstone and his sister took no notice of me, and I spent every day alone, doing nothing.

One day a gentleman visited us. His name was Mr Quinion. Mr Murdstone called me into the room to meet him. "David," he said, "a young boy should not waste time, doing nothing. You must do some useful work. Mr Quinion manages the wine business of Murdstone and Grinby. He is going to take you to London today and give you a job in the storehouse."

So, at the age of ten, I began to work for my living.

Murdstone and Grinby's storehouse stood by the river. The building was very old and almost falling down. The rooms were blackened with the dirt of a hundred years, I dare say.

I worked with four other boys. We had to wash empty bottles; label them for new wine; and put them in wooden cases. The other boys were very rough, and I hated them. I cried as I washed the bottles on my first morning.

The storehouse clock showed half-past twelve — dinner time. Mr Quinion called me into his office. There, I found a fat man with a large shining head: his head had no more hair than an egg has. His clothes were old, but he wore a fine shirt. He carried a stick, and he had an eye-glass that hung round his neck.

"This is Mr Micawber," said Mr Quinion. "He will give you a room in his house."

Mr Micawber told me his address. "I do not suppose you know this city, young sir," he said. "You might lose yourself. I will call this evening at eight o'clock and show you the way." He wished Mr Quinion a good day and left.

Mr Quinion gave me my first week's pay — six shillings*. I gave sixpence to one of the boys to carry my box to Mr Micawber's house: it was too heavy for me.

At eight o'clock in the evening Mr Micawber appeared. He led me to his house. When we arrived, Mrs Micawber — a thin, tired lady — was feeding a baby. There were two other children in the family: a boy and a girl.

Mrs Micawber took me to the top of the house and showed me my room. "I never thought we would have to take money for rooms. But we must make money somehow!" she said. "Poor Mr Micawber is in difficulties. He cannot pay his bills. His troubles are worse every day. I don't know what will happen."

Mrs Micawber put a notice on the front door, offering rooms to 'Homeless Young Ladies'. But no young lady ever came.

The only visitors were men wanting money. They came at all hours — and some were quite angry. At these times, Mr Micawber seemed to be filled with sadness. But he brightened when the men left. He took his stick and went out, happily singing to himself.

* Worth about 30p today.

I liked the Micawbers. I wished I could help them, but I needed every penny of my money for food. I had a piece of bread and some milk for my breakfast. I had dinner at the storehouse: that made a hole in my six shillings! I ate another piece of bread and some cheese for my supper. I was always hungry. I had a very hard time — but Mr Micawber's troubles were worse than mine.

Early one morning a policeman came and took Mr Micawber to prison. I thought his heart would break. But he seemed to be quite happy in prison. One Sunday, I went to see Mr Micawber in prison, and we had dinner together. We sat and talked, laughed and cried.

"Learn a lesson from my difficulties, young friend," said Mr Micawber. "If a man makes twenty pounds a year and saves sixpence, he will be happy. If he spends more than his twenty pounds, he will be in trouble — as I am!

Mr Micawber stayed in prison for many weeks. At last, he was freed.

The Micawbers then decided to leave London and start a fresh life. "We are going to Plymouth, where my family live," Mrs Micawber told me. "My family know a lot of important people there, and they'll find work for my husband."

A week later, the Micawbers left. Sadly, I watched them take their seats on top of the coach. In a minute they were gone.

I went to begin another unhappy day at Murdstone and Grinby's. "I won't work here many more days," I said to myself. I decided to run away — to my aunt, Miss Betsey.

I did not know where Miss Betsey lived. So I wrote to Peggotty and asked her if she knew. She told me that my aunt lived at Dover but she did not know her address. Peggotty sent me some money for the journey — a bright gold coin.

I saw a young man with a little empty cart standing in the road. "Will you take my box to the Dover coach for sixpence?" I asked him.

The young man looked at me and put my box on his cart. "Give me your money," he said in a rough voice.

Hot and excited, I put my hand in my pocket — and my gold coin flew out. The young man caught it. He laughed loudly, jumped on his cart and drove away.

I ran after him but I could not catch him. I lost my box and my money. I felt afraid.

Breathless and crying, I began to walk along the Dover road.

I came to a little old clothes shop. I took off my coat. "Please, sir, will you buy this coat?" I asked the shopkeeper. The man gave me ninepence.

I walked all day. In the evening, I found a field and lay down in some long grass. I slept until the early morning sun woke me.

I continued my journey, and on the second day I walked thirty-five kilometres. I bought some bread and ate my supper by a little river. I washed my tired feet in the river, and then I lay down and slept.

I walked for five days, and slept each night in a bed of grass. At last, I reached Dover.

I asked some fishermen where my aunt lived, but none of them knew. I spent the whole morning trying to find her. Then a kind man with a horse and a cart came along. He pointed up a hill and showed me the way to her house.

I climbed the hill and went into a little shop. "Please, can you tell me where Miss Trotwood lives?" I asked.

A young woman turned round quickly. "I am her servant," she said. "What do you want, boy? Are you trying to get money?"

"Oh, no," I said. "I only want to speak to her, please."

The young woman walked out of the shop. "Follow me!" she said. She led me to a very pretty little house. She left me at the garden gate and hurried into the house.

Almost black with dirt, and afraid, I waited to meet my aunt.

A lady wearing a mob-cap came out of the house. "Go away!" cried Miss Betsey. "No boys here!"

"Please, Miss Trotwood, you are my aunt," I said.

"Oh, God!" cried my aunt.

"I am David Copperfield," I said. "My dear mama has died — and I am very unhappy. I have walked all the way to Dover. I haven't slept in a bed since I began my journey," I broke down and cried.

My aunt caught hold of my neck and took me quickly into the house. She got a bottle and emptied some medicine into my mouth.

"Janet!" she called to her servant. "Heat the bath."

The bath comforted me. After my bath, my aunt tied me up in some great blankets. I expect I was a funny sight. Feeling very hot, I lay on a chair and fell asleep.

When I woke, we had dinner — a hot chicken, followed by fruit cake.

I wondered what my aunt would do with me. But she ate her dinner in silence. After the meal, she and Janet put me to bed in a very nice room.

Next morning, during breakfast, my aunt said suddenly: "I have written to Mr Murdstone! I have ordered him to come here."

"Oh, aunt," I cried. "I can't go back to Mr Murdstone!"

"I don't know what will happen," my aunt said.

Her words filled me with fear. For two days I waited and wondered.

On the afternoon of the second day, my aunt was sitting by the window, sewing. Suddenly she cried out: "Horses on my grass!"

I looked out and saw the Murdstones riding on the grass in front of the house.

Miss Betsey marched out. She pulled the horses off the grass — and marched back again.

Looking a little afraid, Mr Murdstone and his sister entered. "Miss Trotwood," said Mr Murdstone. "This boy is always giving trouble. I gave him a job in a good business. It did not please him. So he ran away and came to you."

"A good business — tut!" said my aunt. "You didn't think of giving the boy any money? Your wife left some money — and a house — and the boy got nothing?"

"My wife left everything to me. She knew I would take care of the boy," Mr Murdstone said.

"H'm! Your wife — poor baby! — had no sense, sir," my aunt returned. "Now what do you say?"

"I have come to take David back," Mr Murdstone replied.

"What does the boy say? Do you wish to go, David?" my aunt asked me.

"Oh, no!" I cried, "I hate Mr Murdstone and his sister. They beat me!"

My aunt pulled me towards her, and said to Mr Murdstone: "Go! I'll keep the boy. Go — and don't ride over my grass again. If you do, I'll — "

The Murdstones walked out of the house. My aunt stood by the window and watched them ride away. She turned and gave me a kind smile.

I put my arms round her neck and kissed her. I never saw the Murdstones again.

Charles Dickens

Illustrated by G.A.S.S.P.

This extract from *David Copperfield* has been shortened and amended slightly by Norman Wymer. You can meet the other interesting characters in David's life if you read the book. There's Uriah Heep, Steerforth, the Wickfields and little Emily who eventually emigrates to Australia with the Micawbers.

Charles Dickens makes us feel the sadness and happiness that David feels. We become involved in David's life and his adventures. In fact, the story Dickens tells is very like his own early life . . . and David Copperfield goes on to become a famous writer!

MEET AN AUTHOR

CHARLES DICKENS

(1812–1870)

CHARLES DICKENS was born in Portsmouth in 1812.

Charles was first taught to read by his mother. He was a very keen reader and he had soon read all the family's books.

The Dickens family moved to London when Charles was twelve. Unfortunately, his father got into debt and was arrested. His mother tried to raise some money to live on by selling spoons, but this was very difficult and so she and the children moved into the prison with their father. As the eldest son, Charles went off to work at a boot-polish factory to earn some money.

When his grandmother died, she left enough money to get the family out of prison and to pay Charles's school fees. He went to the Wellington House Academy in Hampstead, London.

Just before his fifteenth birthday, Charles left school and got a job as a lawyer's clerk. One of his duties was to keep the cash book up to date.

Charles, however, wanted to become a newspaper reporter. So, he taught himself shorthand and started work on a newspaper called *The Mirror of Parliament*.

Charles wrote stories, and his first story to be printed was called 'A Dinner at Poplar Walk', but he didn't get paid for it.

His first book was published in 1836 and it was called *Sketches by Boz*. Boz was his younger brother's nickname.

Charles was now making a profit from writing and so he was able to buy the house of his childhood dreams, at Gad's Hill near Chatham in Kent.

Many films and TV programmes have been adapted from his books. Here is a still from *Oliver*, 1968.

39

What has happened to Lulu?

What has happened to Lulu, mother?
  What has happened to Lu?
There's nothing in her bed but an old rag-doll
  And by its side a shoe.

Why is her window wide, mother,
  The curtain flapping free,
And only a circle on the dusty shelf
  Where her money-box used to be?

Why do you turn your head, mother,
  And why do the tear-drops fall?
And why do you crumple that note on the fire
  And say it is nothing at all?

I woke to voices late last night,
  I heard an engine roar.
Why do you tell me the things I heard
  Were a dream and nothing more?

I heard somebody cry, mother,
  In anger or in pain,
But now I ask you why, mother,
  You say it was a gust of rain.

Why do you wander about as though
  You don't know what to do?

What has happened to Lulu, mother?
  What has happened to Lu?

Charles Causley

THE VOICE THAT CAME WITH THE WIND

Swish . . . swish. The grass moved gently. The frogs froze. What was it?

"May I sleep by the fire and share a little of your food? " asked a voice.

There was nothing to see, but the waving grass. Afraid to say yes, but even more afraid to say no, the frogs made room for their invisible guest. They slept little through the long fearful night, sure that at any moment the unseen stranger would strike.

But morning came and none was harmed. Again the grass moved gently and again a voice spoke:

"I will return before long."

All day, all through the night and into the next day the frogs waited, expecting they knew not what. Perched on tree branches beside the river they watched the grass.

Suddenly a whirlwind rushed towards them, tossing trees and reeds this way and that. It tore through the frogs' camp, spreading ash and live embers from the fire across the sand.

"Don't be afraid", a voice called, but no one was listening. Terrified, sure that the strange spirit had come to kill them, the frogs had leapt into the river and were already hiding deep in its water.

They have never got over their fright. To this day, the slightest movement of the grass or reeds around their waterhole will send them leaping into the water. Only there do they feel safe from the voice that came with the wind.

An Aboriginal story retold and illustrated by Pat Edwards.

43

Why did you run away Margaret Catchpole?

Who was Margaret Catchpole?

Margaret Catchpole was born in 1762, the daughter of a farm labourer living near Ipswich, in Suffolk. Like many girls of her day, she had barely any education. However, what Margaret lacked in reading, writing and arithmetic, she made up for in many ways. At a young age, she galloped bareback on a wild, spirited horse to fetch a doctor to tend a sick neighbour. Twice, she rescued the children of her employer. Not long after, her life took a different turn.

Why did she run away?

Margaret became friendly with a smuggler called William Laud, and in 1797 she supposedly stole a horse and galloped off to London.

Perhaps she had planned to meet William there — no one knows. But she was arrested and sentenced to death for stealing the horse. However, luck must have smiled on her, for the judges changed her death-sentence to seven years' imprisonment.

Margaret Catchpole was in
Ipswich jail for two years,
and then William arrived. He
became a prisoner there too.
Together they planned a
daring escape. They used an
old clothes-line to help hoist
themselves over the prison
wall which was seven metres
high. The guards chased
after them and William was
shot. Margaret was re-arrested
and sent with other convicts
to Australia, where she spent
the rest of her life.

Why do we remember her?

Margaret Catchpole is remembered not for her crimes but
for her courage. After she arrived in Australia in 1801, she
led a varied and interesting life. She ran a small shop and
looked after a farm. She helped women by delivering their
babies. Perhaps it is a fitting end that she died from an
illness caused by going to help a neighbour during bad
weather. Margaret wrote many letters home to England
and these letters say a great deal about life in Sydney,
Australia nearly 200 years ago.

Margaret Catchpole – R.I.P.

Nowhere to run to

Where do you run to if you're sitting in a plane and the pilot suddenly calls out "Down everybody! Heads between knees!"?

Allison quickly obeyed as the small plane plunged and then crashed into the mountainside. Then, everything went black . . .

When she finally came to, Allison discovered that she and her friend Mark were the only ones who could go for help. The other four were too seriously injured.

Bruised and frightened, Allison and Mark move slowly down the dark, unfamiliar mountain. Mark has a broken left arm which is tied in a rough splint made from two sticks. He uses his belt as a sling. Allison carries a flashlight.

"Hey," Mark's voice was a low whisper, "what's that?"

"I don't hear anything —"

"Shhh."

Allison heard it then, soft sounds like somebody barefooted walking over leaves. Except the foot sounds were lighter, closer together than people made. "What is it?"

"Some kind of animal."

"Maybe it's a deer or rabbit."

"No. Listen."

As the sounds approached, she could tell that there were more animals than one. And whatever they were, they were not trying to keep quiet.

Mark's hand shook. "Sounds like a wolf pack."

"Are there wolves here?"

"I don't know. I didn't think so but I don't know."

"We can't just wait here." Allison swung the light in an arc. "Look — down there. It's some kind of clearing. Maybe if we get to it, they won't bother us." Somehow, she didn't know why she thought so, but she believed that if they got to an open area, if they were in a field or something, wolves wouldn't bother them. "Let's go."

The clearing, they discovered when they reached it moments later, was the scarred-over remains of a small forest fire. It was about the size of a tennis court, except that it was bulged in the middle and the edges were ragged. "Wonder why it stopped burning?"

Mark stared about. "Rain put it out, I bet —"

He stopped abruptly as they both heard a new and different sound. "You hear that?"

"Sounds like — hey," Allison said, forgetting the animals, "it's a plane!"

"They're already looking!" Mark gripped her hand tighter and led her to the middle of the clearing. "The light — point it up!"

Without stopping to think about the stubble of trunks and charred branches, Allison swung the flashlight upward — and let it slip from her hand. She cried out and dropped to her knees, ignoring the blackened rubble. Frantically, she rummaged through the loose covering, clutching once at a short stub of branch, grabbing again at a burned-over root.

"It's coming closer — hurry.!"

She did not want to but she couldn't keep from crying as she scratched and dug through the debris. The plane passed overhead, moving west to east, its lights tracing a straight line through the blackened sky. "We're here! We're right here!" she screamed.

The lights disappeared just as she found the flashlight.

"Gone," Mark said slowly. His voice had a catch in it.

"But if they're looking," and Allison turned on the light and wildly waved its beam through the darkness, "they'll come back! They have to!"

It did. From somewhere to the east of them, they heard the changing sound of the engine as the search plane turned, flew east to west, though farther south this time, then once more west to east. On both those passes, however, it was well beyond the foothills, probably, Allison guessed, over the flat land they'd seen before the crash. "Dumb. Dumb, dumb, dumb," she said softly.

"You didn't mean to drop it," Mark told her. "Besides, even if they'd seen it, they wouldn't know what it was." He sniffed hard. "And that thing's not working."

"What thing?"

"You know — that ELT*."

"How do you know?"

"They were right over it — close enough, anyway."

"But they'll be back. You know they won't give up after just one try."

Mark caught the belt sling and tried to shift his arm. "They may not come back this way, though."

Through his hand, once more clutching hers, Allison felt a shudder pass though him. She wanted to sit down right there, wanted to cup her face in her hands and cry. The little wrist-watch told her it was after seven o'clock. Too dark. Too damp out here on this mountainside —

"Allison!" Once more Mark's voice was low and tight. "They're still close."

She tensed, caught her breath, and listened hard. To her left, somewhere in the woods, the animal footsteps seemed closer now. She could not tell how many there were, but the sounds gave her to believe there were more than two. "I — I think they're coming this way."

"I know they are."

Suddenly one of them gave a little yelp and Mark's hand trembled. "Not wolves," he whispered.

"What?"

"Dogs — wild dogs."

"Where'd they come from?"

* Emergency Locator Transmitter — a small machine which sends out special signals that can be picked up on radio receivers (see p. 58).

"Lost, maybe. Runaways. Dumped in the woods. Now they're a wild pack. Worse than wolves."

"They won't hurt us, will they?"

"Can't ever tell. They go into farmers' yards at night, kill their chickens. Sometimes they even attack little calves."

A twig broke, then another, and just as Allison turned the light to her left, the sounds suddenly died. "Oh!"

"Wait — don't move."

Four, no, there were five of them, five dogs of varying sizes broke out of the woods and stopped at the far edge of the clearing. The light beam shifted from one to the other, reflecting greenish glows as it shone in their eyes. "Mark — "

"Shhh," he whispered once more. "Don't move."

Allison couldn't be sure, but the leader looked much like a German shepherd, except that its coat seemed to be black with splotches of tan. Its long ears were up, and its tongue seemed to roll out the side of its mouth. "What're they going to do?"

"I — I don't know."

"Will they attack us?"

"They might."

For a moment the dogs stood in a line, as if they were surprised to see people in the woods. Then the smallest one — Allison couldn't be certain what kind it was except that it had short hair and floppy ears — darted to one side, nipped at the leg of a slightly larger dog, then yelped as the other nipped back. The rest began milling side to side, while the leader seemed to ease forward.

"Get away! Get" Mark shouted.

The dogs froze in place, as if startled by the sound of his voice, then began moving once more, this time one, then another, barking.

Allison squatted down, aimed the light at the ground, and searched for a stick.

"What're you doing?"

"We have to hit them or run them off."

"Stay still — maybe they won't come any closer. But keep the light in their eyes."

Without rising, Allison aimed the beam again. In that brief instant she realized they had come halfway from the clearing's edge toward them. "I'm afraid."

"Me, too. But we can't let them know it."

"Get! Get away, dogs!"

Her voice, higher-pitched than Mark's, seemed to surprise the animals. The leader stopped short, poised itself in a half crouch, laid its ears back, and showed its teeth.

"Mark!"

"I see," he whispered. "Just don't move a muscle."

Still squatting, Allison aimed the light directly into the big dog's face. Its eyes gleamed like two round reflectors, its neck seemed rigid, and its mouth was half parted. "But we can't just stay here."

"We can't leave."

"What are we going to do?" She played the light from one to the other for a brief moment, then once again pointed it at the leader. The others, she noticed, were half milling about, half staying just behind the big one, as if awaiting a signal. Perhaps a rush at them? "Why can't we just run?"

"There's nothing to run to."

"If we went back to the plane — "

"It'd be easier to run downhill." Slowly he lowered himself until he was almost kneeling right beside her. "Reach behind you — no, don't let the light move, keep it right on him. Now — do you feel anything, a stick, maybe a rock?"

"Nothing." Her fingers groped in the dark, touched burned leaves, loose dirt, burned-over twigs. But nothing big and solid.

"Well, ease away from me — no, not like that, slow. Real slow. Now. Feel again."

Stretching back as far as she could, Allison once more groped for some kind of object, anything. Finally, her fingers touched what she imagined to be a length of burned branch. "A stick. I've got a stick."

"Can you tell how long it is?"

"No."

"Well, drag it anyway. Be careful, don't make any noise — hey, easy!"

The limb was almost as long as her arm, its surface charred, and its end almost pointed. Gingerly, she eased it over the ground, not daring to raise it, and shoved it toward Mark. "This is all I can find."

Cautiously, he stretched out his right arm, caught the stick, and pulled it closer, "Anything else?"

"I'll see." Once more she fumbled in the ashes and once more her hand came upon something large and round.

Moving her fingers over it, she realized it was a stone, almost as big as an orange. "Got a rock."

"Good. Hand it." Keeping his own hands in the dark, out of the way of the light's beam, he took the rock and shoved the stick toward her left side. "You take this."

"What're you going to do?"

"I'll throw it at the far side — "

"Maybe you won't hit him."

"I'm not going to try to hit him. But if I can make noise behind them, maybe they'll get scared."

"What if they don't?"

"If they attack, you'll just have to use the stick."

"I don't know."

"We have to." Very slowly, he raised himself and poised for the throw. "Ready?"

"I guess." She grasped the stick and carefully turned so she could hold it as a club. "But I hope they run."

"One thing more — if they start toward us, don't turn your back. Okay?"

"Okay." But she could not keep from shaking all over.

"Now — one, two — three!" He yelled the last word as loud as he could, then hurled the rock over the animals' heads. It struck the trunk of a tree, made a dull, thumping sound, then crashed into what sounded like a pile of brittle bushes. The smallest dog yelped, sprang straight up, then whirled about, and took off down the hill, with two others barking behind him. But the leader did not follow. Instead, it crouched lower, as did the other big animal, the one Allison thought looked a little like an Airedale. Then with a sudden snarl, they sprang forward.

"Mark!"

"I see them!" he yelled . . .

The moment she saw them make their first move, Allison stood and swapped the light and stick so she could swing with her right arm. But for some reason, both animals charged at Mark. She hesitated only an instant, then brought the club around and swung it as hard as she could toward the nearest dog. The Airedale yelped and wheeled as the stick crashed across its backside. It drew up, crouched once more, then poised as if to spring at Allison. She screamed and once more swung at it.

53

54

This time, the stick broke across the animal's shoulder, and again it yelped. As it fell to the side, it rolled over, pawed the loose ashes, and bounced once more to its feet. Allison stared at the stub in her hand and screamed, "Get away, get away!"

"Allison!"

She whirled. The German shepherd had its jaws clamped on Mark's right arm and was trying to pull back, Mark was screaming and kicking at it, stumbling backward and trying to keep his left out of the animal's way. "Hit him, hit him!"

Allison threw the broken remnant at the dog, missed it, hesitated for a brief instant, then clubbed its head with the flashlight.

The dog yelped and released Mark's arm. Whirling, it started to spring at her. Mark yelled at her to dodge, then kicked out. His foot caught the animal in its side, sending it rolling over as the Airedale had done. Unlike the Airedale, however, the German shepherd bounded to its feet, spun about, and once more charged him. Mark screamed as the sling slipped from his arm, but he pointed his left hand in the dog's direction. As it sprang toward him, its teeth bared, the projecting stub of the splint caught it full on the end of its head.

Abruptly, it dropped to the ground, pawed violently at its nose, and backed away, still crouching.

"Run!" Mark yelled. "Now!"

Allison spun about, the flashlight cutting wild arcs in the darkness, and scrambled to the edge of the clearing, with Mark right behind her. For a moment she knew the dogs would chase after them, but when she reached the first of the huge trees, paused and looked back, the Airedale was ambling off toward the far side. The German shepherd was sitting in the clearing, still trying to rub the tip of its nose with a forepaw.

Mark stopped at the first big tree he came to, leaned against it, and clutched his left arm with his right hand. When Allison turned the light on him, she saw that his coat was torn at the sleeve, the belt was dangling from his neck, and the splints were twisted out of place. She also saw that Mark was crying. "Did he bite you?"

Mark nodded and indicated his right wrist.

"Let's see," and she moved closer. Pushing his sleeve up, she saw red marks where the teeth had dug in. But she saw no blood. "I don't think he broke the skin."

"I thought he did." Mark tried to drag his arm across his face, blotting at the tears. "Put your light on it."

She did as he told her. "Guess it's lucky you had on the thick jacket."

Mark sniffed and nodded, then slowly clutched his left arm. "But this one hurts." He turned it, winced, then glanced back toward the clearing. The German shepherd was still sitting, still trying to paw its nose.

56

"I hope he leaves us alone."

"Do you think he'll attack us again?"

"I don't know. Never can tell." He slowly raised the arm, letting the elbow bend, gritting his teeth at the pain. "I just hope he won't go up there."

Allison caught her breath. "You don't think they'll go —"

Just then one of the three that had run off set to barking. The Airedale loped off in the direction of the sound, and slowly the shepherd rose and followed.

Hilary Milton
Illustrated by
Don Black

57

Fascinating facts about signalling

In the story "Nowhere to run to", Mark and Allison were very foolish to have left the scene of the crash. Instead of going to look for help, they should have stayed put and let help come to them!

Mark was carrying an ELT — an Emergency Locator Transmitter, also called an Emergency Locator Beacon. Small planes sometimes carry portable ELTs, but it's more common for an ELT to be built into the aircraft's body. Then, if the aircraft should crash, a special "bump" switch turns on the ELT. For the next 72–96 hours the ELT transmits a signal. This signal is not heard by people at the site of the crash, but it can be picked up on aircraft radio receivers up to 150 kilometres away!

From earliest times, people have needed ways to send a message *quickly* — without the need for someone to carry that message. Smoke, drums, fires, and the reflection of sunlight, have all been used to send signals. But the development of electricity and the invention of the telegraph completely changed our ways of sending signals by sound.

Samuel Finley Breese Morse not only had a wonderful name, but most importantly, a remarkably inventive brain! He spent his days trying to find a way to transmit messages. (And he wasn't into letter writing!) His dedication was rewarded. By 1837 he had invented and patented the electric telegraph, now known as "Morse Code". In 1844, he sent a telegraphic message from Washington DC to Baltimore in the USA — a distance of about 60 kilometres, covered in a matter of seconds.

dit-dit-dit- dar- dar- dar- dit-dit-dit

The Morse Code is made up of a series of dots and dashes, and is designed to be heard rather than seen, so the following message . . . ——— . . . would sound something like this: dit-dit-dit dar dar dar dit-dit-dit.

It is spelling out "S.O.S." which means "save our souls". This distress signal was often used in times of war.

If you were on board a sinking ship, or an aircraft that was in difficulty, you would send out a "Mayday" call. The Mayday signal is a radio telephonic distress signal. It has nothing to do with the "merry month of May". Mayday is the English version of two French words "M'aidez". It sounds exactly the same and means "Help me!".

The Map-Makers

It's amazing how often we all use maps. Imagine trying to find your way around a big city without a street map, or across Britain without a road map? Whether driving a car or navigating a ship or plane, a map is essential. You'll also find maps on railway stations and street corners, and in parks and supermarkets. In fact, they are one of the handiest inventions we have.

So who invented maps?

Well, that's a hard one to answer. We know who drew the first map of the world. He was a Greek astronomer named Anaximander who lived around 6 BC. It's believed Anaximander also invented the sundial and that he was first to work out how to calculate the equinoxes (the times each year when night and day are equal in length) and the solstices (the shortest and longest days and nights). However, Anaximander's map wouldn't be much use today because he believed the earth was flat — and of course, he included only the world as he knew it, the area around the Mediterranean.

In those times, people who travelled by sea were very nervous about falling over the edge of the earth and down into endless space. It was a terrifying thought, worse even than that of being swallowed by one of the huge sea monsters that were said to lurk beneath the waves. It was best to stay in sight of land.

Time passed. Bigger and safer ships were built. Sailors became bolder and travelled further and further. Both the Chinese and the Greeks had been experimenting with the lodestone (a mineral which can be used as a magnet). Other people learned from them, and finally a magnetic compass was invented by a Frenchman in AD 1269. It was therefore possible for travellers to find their way home much more easily, and traders and explorers travelled even further. They turned their eyes to the far horizon, wondering what exciting sights and riches were across the mountain ranges or rolling seas. But they needed compasses and maps to take along with them.

61

During the 1500s, people began to realize that the earth was a
sphere, not a flat dish. Because it is like a sphere, the earth's correct
shape can only be shown on a globe. Because maps and charts are
flat, cartographers, as map-makers are called, had to work out a way
of showing the round earth as accurately as possible on a flat map.

They divided the earth along lines which are called lines of latitude
and lines of longitude. These lines are imaginary — you can't go out
and find them marked on the earth's surface. Lines of longitude join
the north and south poles and are *not* parallel to each other. Lines of
latitude run around the earth and *are* parallel to each other.

By using lines of latitude and longitude we can work out the
position of any place on the earth.

If you are being tossed around far out at sea, you might want to
know how close is the nearest land. By calculating to which lines of
latitude and longitude you are near, you can work out how close you
are to land.

The exact position of continents and islands can be given using
latitude and longitude and this helps navigators work out where they are.

The way in which the curved lines of latitude and longitude on the
globe are drawn on a flat map depends on the type of map projection
that is used.

On some map projections latitude and longitude are drawn as curves,
on others they are drawn as straight lines.

Who was Ptolemy?

A Greek astronomer and geographer who lived around AD 90–168. He worked out that the earth was a sphere and he used lines of latitude and longitude on his maps, very like the lines we use today!

Who was Mercator?

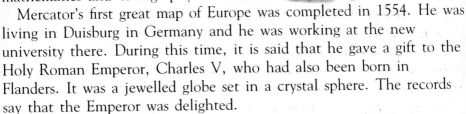

Mercator wasn't his real name. He was born on 5th March 1512 in Flanders (now part of Belgium) and he was called Gerhard Kremer. It is thought that his parents were German. Mercator is the Latin name he used on his maps and in his books.

When Mercator was only ten, he heard of wonderful voyages around the world. Perhaps it was these stories that made him decide to study mathematics and cartography.

Mercator's first great map of Europe was completed in 1554. He was living in Duisburg in Germany and he was working at the new university there. During this time, it is said that he gave a gift to the Holy Roman Emperor, Charles V, who had also been born in Flanders. It was a jewelled globe set in a crystal sphere. The records say that the Emperor was delighted.

The first part of his famous atlas began to appear in 1585. It was to take ten years to complete, but Mercator did not live to see this. He died at the age of 82 in 1594. His son Rumold finished the maps that were to help seamen roam the world.

His book of maps was the first to be called an "atlas". Why? Because it had a picture of the Greek god, Atlas, supporting the earth on its cover!

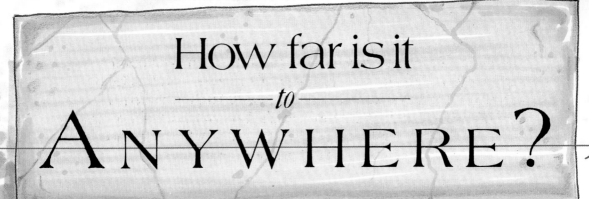

How far is it to ANYWHERE?

Distance over land is always given in kilometres. Once you know that kilo comes from the Greek word meaning "thousand" it's easy to work out that a kilometre is made up of one thousand metres. The word metre comes from a Greek word meaning "measure".

However, in Britain and in some other countries distance was given in miles for quite a long time. The word "mile" has quite an interesting history.

When the Greek and Roman cartographers were drawing up their maps they employed official "pacers" — men who paced out the distance from one place to another. The Roman pace was the length of a double step; that is, the distance moved by one foot from the time it left the ground until it was placed down again.

The word "mile" also means a "thousand". It comes from the Latin word *mille* and that's just what a mile was — a thousand paces. Its length was changed several times through the ages, but it was still called a mile. One mile equals 1.6 kilometres. There are also sea miles (or nautical miles) which are slightly longer than land miles. One nautical mile equals 1.15 land miles.

Instead of measuring speed according to miles (or kilometres) per hour, sailors still talk about knots. One knot equals one nautical mile per hour. But why do we call them knots?

In the olden days sailors used a line, called a log-line, to measure the speed of their ships. The log-line had a heavy wooden float, or log, attached to one end. When a sailor wanted to measure his ship's speed, he threw the log overboard. The log floated and the line unwound from a reel.

The line had knots tied in it and the distance between each knot was $\frac{1}{120}$ of a nautical mile. There are 120 half-minutes in one hour, and so by counting the number of knots that left the reel in half a minute the sailor could measure the speed. If one knot passed in half a minute it would indicate that $\frac{1}{120}$ of a nautical mile had been covered in $\frac{1}{120}$ of an hour. In other words, the ship would be travelling at 1 nautical mile per hour. If six knots passed, the ship would be travelling at 6 nautical miles per hour.

Today, a ship's "speedometer" is still called the "log"!

A Narrow escape

Bambi, a young deer, has been living happily in the forest with his friends. He is quite unaware of men and guns . . .

One morning Bambi came to grief.

The pale grey dawn was just creeping through the forest. A milky-white mist was rising from the meadow and the stillness that precedes the coming of light was everywhere. The crows were not awake yet, nor the magpies. The jays were asleep . . .

Bambi stood under the great oak at the meadow's edge and peered out cautiously drinking in the pure and odourless morning air. It was moist and fresh from the earth, the dew, the grass and the wet woods. He breathed in great gulps of it. All at once his spirit felt freer than for a long time. He walked happily on to the mist-covered meadow.

Then a sound like thunder crashed.

Bambi felt a fearful blow that made him stagger.

Mad with terror, he sprang back into the thicket and kept running. He did not understand what had happened. He could not grasp a single idea. He could only keep running on and on. Fear gripped his heart so that his breath failed as he rushed blindly on. Then a killing pain shot through him, so that he felt that he could not bear it. He felt something hot running over his left shoulder. It was like a thin burning thread coming from where the pain shot through him. Bambi had to stop running. He was forced to walk slower. Then he saw that he was limping. He sank down.

It was comfortable just to lie there and rest.

"Up, Bambi! Get up!" the old stag was standing beside him and nudging his shoulder gently.

Bambi wanted to answer "I can't," but the old stag repeated, "Up! Up!". And there was such compulsion in his voice and such tenderness that Bambi kept silent. Even the pain that shot through him stopped for a minute.

Then the old stag said hurriedly and anxiously, "Get up! You must get away, my son." My son! The words seemed to have escaped him. In a flash Bambi was on his feet.

"Good," said the old stag, breathing deeply and speaking emphatically, "come with me now and keep close beside me."

He walked swiftly ahead. Bambi followed him, but he felt a burning desire to let himself drop to the ground, to lie still and rest.

The old stag seemed to guess it and talked to him without stopping. "Now you'll have to bear every pain. You can't think of lying down now. You mustn't think of it even for a moment. That's enough to tire you in itself. You must save yourself; do you understand me, Bambi? Save yourself; or else you are lost. Just remember that He is behind you; do you understand, Bambi? And He will kill you without mercy. Come on. Keep close to me. You'll soon be all right. You must be all right."

Bambi had no strength left to think with. The pain shot through him at every step he took. It took away his breath and his consciousness. The hot trickle, burning his shoulder, seared him like some deep heartfelt trouble.

The old stag made a wide circle. It took a long time. Through his veil of pain and weakness, Bambi was amazed to see that they were passing the great oak again.

The old stag stopped and snuffed the ground. "He's still here," he whispered. "It's He. And that's His dog. Come along. Faster!" They ran.

Suddenly the old stag stopped again. "Look," he said, "that's where you lay on the ground."

Bambi saw the crushed grasses where a wide pool of his own blood was soaking into the earth.

The old stag snuffed warily around the spot. "They were here, He and His dog," he said. "Come along!" He went ahead slowly, snuffing again and again.

Bambi saw the red drops gleaming on the leaves of the bushes and the grass stems. "We passed here before," he thought. But he couldn't speak.

"Aha!" said the old stag, and seemed almost joyful, "we're behind them now."

He continued for a while on the same path. Then he doubled unexpectedly and began a new circle. Bambi staggered after him. They came to the oak again but on the opposite side. For the second time they passed the place where Bambi had fallen down. Then the old stag went in still another direction.

"Eat that," he commanded suddenly, stopping and pushing aside the grasses. He pointed to a pair of short dark-green leaves growing close together near the ground.

Bambi obeyed. They tasted terribly bitter and smelt sickeningly.

"How do you feel now?" the stag asked after a while.

"Better," Bambi answered quickly. He was suddenly able to speak again. His senses had cleared and his fatigue grew less.

"Let's move on again," the old stag commanded after another pause. After Bambi had been following him for a long time he said, "At last!" They stopped.

"The bleeding has stopped," said the old stag, "the blood's stopped flowing from your wound. It isn't emptying your veins now. And it can't betray you any more either. It can't show Him and His dog where to find you and kill you."

The old stag looked worried and tired but his voice sounded joyful. "Come along," he went on, "now you can rest."

They reached a wide ditch which Bambi had never crossed. The old stag climbed down and Bambi tried to follow him. But it cost him a great effort to climb the steep slope on the farther side. The pain began to shoot violently through him again. He stumbled, regained his feet, and stumbled again, breathing hard.

"I can't help you," said the old stag, "you'll have to get up yourself." Bambi reached the top. He felt the hot trickle on his shoulder again. He felt his strength ebbing for the second time.

"You're bleeding again," said the old stag. "I thought you would, but it's only a little," he added in a whisper, "and it doesn't make any difference now."

They walked very slowly through a grove of lofty beeches. The ground was soft and level. They walked easily on it. Bambi felt a longing to lie down there, to stretch out and never move his limbs again. He couldn't go any farther. His head ached. There was a humming in his ears. His nerves were quivering, and fever began to rack him. There was a darkness before his eyes. He felt nothing but a desire for rest and a detached amazement at finding his life so changed and shattered. He remembered how he had walked whole and uninjured through the woods that morning. It was barely an hour ago, and it seemed to him like some memory out of a distant, long-vanished past.

They passed through a scrub-oak and dogwood thicket. A huge, hollow beech-trunk, thickly entangled with the bushes, lay right in front of them, barring the way.

"Here we are," Bambi heard the old stag saying. He walked along the beech-trunk and Bambi walked beside him. He nearly fell into a hollow that lay in front of him.

"Here it is," said the old stag at the moment; "you can lie down here."

Bambi sank down and did not move again.

The hollow was still deeper under the beech-trunk and formed a little chamber. The bushes closed thickly across the top so whoever was within lay hidden.

"You'll be safe here," said the old stag.

Days passed.

Bambi lay on the warm earth with the mouldering bark of the fallen tree above him. He felt his pain intensify and then grow less and less until it died away more and more gently.

Sometimes he would creep out and stand swaying weakly on his unsteady legs. He would take a few stiff steps to look for food. He ate plants now that he had never noticed before. Now they appealed to his taste and attracted him by their strange enticing acrid smell. Everything that he had disdained before and would spit out if it got accidentally into his mouth, seemed appetizing to him. He still disliked many of the little leaves and short, coarse shoots; but he ate them anyway as though he were compelled to, and his wound healed faster. He felt his strength returning.

He was cured, but he didn't leave the hollow yet. He walked around a little at night, but lay quietly on his bed by day. Not until the fever had entirely left his body did Bambi begin to think over all that had happened to him. Then a great terror awoke in him, and a profound tremor passed through his heart. He could not shake himself free of it. He could not get up and run about as before. He lay still and troubled. He felt terrified, ashamed, amazed and troubled by turns. Sometimes he was full of despair, at others of joy.

The old stag was always with him. At first he stayed day and night at Bambi's side. Then he left him alone at times, especially when he saw Bambi deep in thought. But he always kept close at hand.

One night there was thunder and lightning and a downpour of rain, although the sky was clear and the setting sun was streaming down. The blackbirds sang loudly in all the neighbouring tree-tops, the finches warbled, the field-mice chirped in the bushes. Among the grasses or from under the bushes, the metallic, throaty cackling of the pheasants sounded at intervals. The woodpecker laughed exultantly and the doves cooed their fervid love.

Bambi crept out of the hollow. Life was beautiful. The old stag was standing there as though he expected Bambi. They sauntered on together. And Bambi did not return to the hollow again.

Felix Salten
Illustrated by G.A.S.S.P

Meeting

As I went home on the old wood road,
   With my basket and lesson book,
A deer came out of the tall trees
   And down to drink at the brook.

Twilight was all about us,
   Twilight and tree on tree;
I looked straight into its great, strange eyes,
   And the deer looked back at me.

Beautiful, brown, and unafraid,
   Those eyes returned my stare;
And something with neither sound nor name
   Passed between us there.

Something I shall not forget —
   Something still, and shy, and wise —
In the dimness of the woods
   From a pair of gold-flecked eyes.

Rachel Field

New Zealand

There was a major goldrush in Australia in the 1850s — people were in search of gold. By 1860 most of the gold had been found. This forced goldminers to move on to look for gold in other regions of Australia and in New Zealand. In 1861 a large goldfield was discovered at Gabriel's Gully in the South Island of New Zealand.

NORTH ISLAND

Auckland

Bay of Plenty

North Taranaki Bight

Wellington

Cook Strait

PACIFIC OCEAN

0 50 100 150 200 250 km

TASMAN SEA

SOUTHERN ALPS

SOUTH ISLAND

Christchurch

Canterbury Bight

Clutha R.

Dunedin

Invercargill

Foveaux Strait

STEWART I.

166° 168° 170° 172° 174° 176°

Clutha

Gabriel's Gully

Dunedin

River

In search of GOLD

Life for a gold-digger was anything but glamorous. You had to work long and hard for a few grams of gold. Then you had to hide it from your "mates", and always you were trying to keep ahead, searching for new claims and trying to keep them secret for as long as you could, before others caught up with you.

Johnie is 14. He is digging for gold at Gabriels Gully, near the Clutha River in New Zealand's South Island. He has teamed up with an old digger, called Tatey. Gold is running out and Tatey has sneaked off in search of a new claim, leaving Johnie in charge and trying hard to keep Tatey's disappearance a secret from their "mates", Dan and Rex.

Nobody worked their gold claims on Sundays, so it was Sunday evening when Dan called in to see whether Tatey would come for a game of cards, before he was missed.

"Where is he?" Dan wanted to know.

"Gone for wood," I said. By this time I was becoming as used to lies as my companions.

"I thought you carried the wood and water around here," Dan said. He went away without suspecting, but in the morning he knew, by some means of his own and came back to see me.

"So he's gone prospecting," he said, and I could not deny it.

"Which direction did he go?"

I pointed in the direction he had gone.

"You're getting just as foxy as he is," Dan said. His eyes flashed with annoyance and he went away immediately.

I settled down to passing dirt through the cradle. It's an absorbing occupation, shovelling in the dirt, pouring water over it, rocking it back and forth, wash, wash, wash. You never know what will turn up on the bottom, and the first week Tatey was away I washed out two ounces*, which would bring in about seven pounds in cash when it was sold, and there was no danger that week that Tatey would gamble it away. I buried it in the hole under my bed, and covered it with a flat stone.

I had just stood up from doing this when Dan appeared at the tent flap with something in a white cloth for me.

"Some damper," he said. "I made it in the camp oven. Are you looking after yourself while Tatey Scone is away?"

* about 56 grams

"We've got a camp oven now, too," I told him. 'Some men who were going home didn't want to take it with them."

"I should think not," Dan said. "An iron pot like that!"

"Tatey does the cooking," I told him. "I made myself a stew from mutton chops and I made so much I've been eating it all week. I didn't know how much to make. I didn't know you could make bread in it." I began to eat the damper he had brought me because I was always hungry.

"You know it's not bread," Dan said, "there's no yeast in it —"

"This is good enough for me," I said.

"Come over to our tent in the morning and I'll show you how to make it," Dan said. "You're sticking mighty close to this tent. Expecting Tatey back soon, are you?"

"I don't know when he's coming back."

"How many weeks' provisions did he take?"

"Tatey doesn't tell me everything."

"I can believe that," Dan said. "He's a sly old fox. He's got a great nose for smelling out gold and he got plenty in Victoria but he'd gamble the shirt off his back. You'll never get rich in his company. Easy come and easy go."

"I wouldn't call digging for gold easy," I said.

"You're too young, that's why," Dan said.

"I'm not so young as I was," I countered. "I'm pretty strong." And I rolled up my sleeve and showed off the muscles I had developed in my arm since I had been digging for gold. . . . And he went off laughing. He was always a great tease.

In the morning I went to his tent to watch him make damper. He made it in a gold-pan, throwing in four mugs of flour, and adding salt, baking soda, cream of tartar and water. He kneaded the dough and cooked it in his heated camp oven by keeping fire hot on the lid of the iron pot as well as underneath. He showed me the best kind of wood to use and where I could get it. So I went away up the head of the gully looking for wood.

I was away for some hours and when I came back, dragging the wood, I saw at once that the tent had been disturbed. I had left it laced and now it was flapping open. My first thought was for the gold I had hidden under my bed, and when I looked I saw that it was gone.

Of course I suspected Dan had taken it, since he knew I had gone for wood. But anyone at all could have seen me go up the gully, and as Tatey had been away for a week everyone knew he was away prospecting. I had noticed miners watching the tent and had concluded that they were waiting for Tatey's return. I now remembered that Dan had told me not to hide gold in an obvious place, such as under my bed or under the fireplace, and this seemed to point to his innocence. But Rex had been present when Dan had been showing me how to make damper and telling me where to go for wood, and Rex was a silent, watchful man, who constantly ignored me. Why suspect Dan and not Rex?

My thoughts raced round in my head, wondering whether I should tell Dan or not tell Dan, blaming myself for not hiding the gold in a better place, growing full of anger against the person who had taken the gold that had cost me a hard week's work, and, most of all, blaming myself for leaving the camp at all. I also felt that I had let Tatey down, because he had left me in charge and told me to look after the tent and the claim, and when he came back I would have no gold to show him, just as though I had loafed the whole week.

I grew very miserable after an hour or two of these thoughts and realized that there was nothing at all I could do as I hadn't a shred of proof against anyone. And even if I could find out who had my gold what could a boy do against men? It was true, as Dan had always told me, I was too young for the goldfields.

80

In this mood of despondency I went to bed without bothering to eat anything, having lost my appetite, and shed a few tears into the red scarf my mother had knitted for me, before falling asleep.

I was awakened by a slight sound outside the tent when it was still dark. A black figure filled the tent-opening and approached me and I sat up, terrified, thinking someone was going to kill me.

"Not a sound!" hissed a voice. It was Tatey.

My heart was banging so loudly that I thought he must hear it.

"Johnie!" He moved close to my ear. "I've found gold. I had to wait till it was dark to come in. I don't want to be followed. Get up and put on all the warm clothes you've got. Spread out your blanket and put in all the food. We'll take the frying pan and not another thing. I've left my gear over the hills. We'll leave the tent standing — everything. Just take what you can carry. I'm going to carry the cradle."

"It's too heavy," I whispered, awed by his whispering voice, and sensing his excitement.

"There's no coming back," Tatey said. "What we take now is all we're going to have. So use your wits."

"I had two ounces of gold," I told him, "and someone has taken it."

After a moment's pause Tatey said, "That's chicken-feed where we're going."

When I heard that, all my troubles fell away from me. I got up in the greatest of excitement and bundled up a heavy swag as Tatey directed me, all in no more light than came from the moon and stars, and like two shadows we stole away from Gabriels Gully, with Tatey actually carrying the heavy gold-cradle on his back. We left our tent standing as though still occupied.

Travelling by night was very slow, but gradually the sky lightened and the sun came up in a clear sky and shone on the tops of the hills that surrounded us. There was no road, no track, no fence, no house, no tree in that lonely landscape. The only vegetation was the New Zealand tussock and thorny bushes which grew among great rough rocks.

Tatey wanted to put the greatest distance possible between ourselves and the gully we had left, so we kept on till I felt my legs trembling from hunger and weariness and asked him when we were going to have breakfast. We had climbed down into a pass, by that time, where a little stream ran over stones, and there, hidden between two great rocks as big as houses, we fried some bacon in the pan and then boiled water in the same pan and drank it scalding hot. Tatey took care to hide the evidence of our fire and we pressed on, sleeping that night in the tussocks in the shelter of rocks.

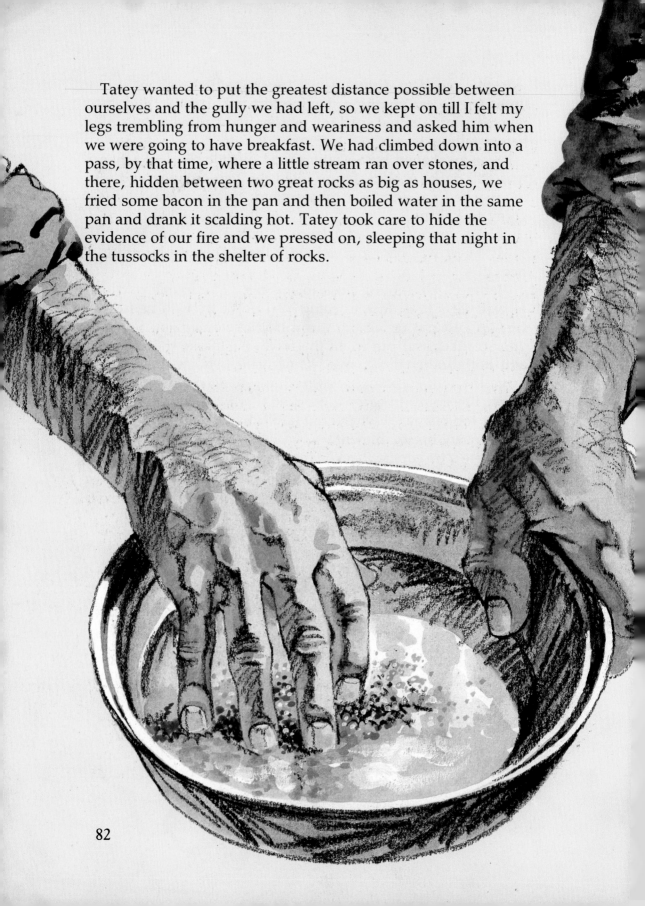

Rocks had become the main feature of the landscape, some standing in clusters as though meeting to discuss the intrusion of two fly-like human beings on their territory. Some were in long ridges, like petrified railway carriages. Some had mats of tussock on their heads like wigs. It was desert country, steep country, a mad kind of country, only fit for madmen in search of gold.

Tatey was a little ahead of me. I was tramping along behind him. At the top of a hill he paused and told me to look down. In the next valley I could see the gleam of water like a knife blade. A stream wound along the valley floor, a mere ribbon of water, running over a wide area of bare mountain shingle, sometimes hidden, and sometimes showing up further on.

"No one's been here," Tatey said, "ever." And he began to hurry down the steep hillside as though in competition with other men who might reach the stream first.

"This is the spot," he said, setting down the cradle at the waterside. I, too, set down my swag, and was very glad to do so. I could see no sign of Tatey's having staked out a claim, or of a pit where he had been digging. The stony valley was bare and desolate and we were enclosed by a complete circle of bare hills. The water made a musical sound as it ran over the stones. To my great amazement Tatey seized the frying pan and walked into the water without taking his boots off, and, with his bare hands, began to scoop gravel from the bottom of the river into the pan, and to wash it, where he stood. Then he carried the pan out to me and I could see gold shining on the bottom as though it had been spilt there.

We stared at the gold and looked into each other's faces, neither of us able to speak. I had imagined that men jumped for joy when they found gold. Instead, I found tears blurring my vision.

"There's a bar," Tatey said at last, "a river bar — it's caught on the bar — every time I put down my shovel —"

He set up the cradle and fell to feeding it with river gravel and water and rocking it with my enthusiastic assistance and before long we had washed up nearly two ounces.

I couldn't understand this method of mining gold. I thought it had to be dug out of a hole in the ground and I told Tatey so.

"If it's been buried by floods since the beginning of time, of course you have to dig for it," Tatey said. "That's how we got it in Victoria. But this is not Australia, it's New Zealand, and if we're going to get gold in the rivers as well as in the ground our fortune's made."

When the sun disappeared behind the hills the valley grew very cold and I asked Tatey if his feet were not cold, since his boots and trouser legs were wet and he was still walking in and out of the river.

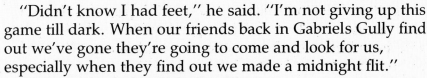

"Didn't know I had feet," he said. "I'm not giving up this game till dark. When our friends back in Gabriels Gully find out we've gone they're going to come and look for us, especially when they find out we made a midnight flit."

"Do you think they'll find us?"

"I'm not waiting to see," Tatey said. "I'm going to scratch up and down this river while the going's good. And turn out first thing in the morning, too, use all the hours of daylight. If we get a rush we'll be confined to a twenty-four foot* claim and our fortune will be gone."

At length it grew too dark to see what we were doing, so we retired to a sheltered place among the rocks that jutted from the foot of the hillside, where Tatey had left his calico tent and other gear he had taken on his prospecting trip. We built a fire from sticks we had gathered in the river bed and cooked a meal and Tatey dried his wet boots on warmed stones.

Those were the last days of autumn, sunny and short, with clear blue skies, and with a full moon at night, and stars sparkling in the first light frosts. I kept my clothes on for warmth and rolled myself in my blanket. When I closed my eyes I saw gold, flakes, crumbs, nuggets. Tatey had estimated that we had washed up about five ounces.

"Where are we going to hide it?" I asked him.

"Where you'd least expect to find it," he said. "We'll think of something." Then he said, "To think it was lying here all the time while we were working like convicts back at Gabriels! It's been lying here for centuries!"

"Has this valley got a name?"

"You name it."

I fell asleep trying to think of a name for it, but in the morning noticed a tall rock that was like the chimney that is left standing when a house has been burnt down, and called it Chimney Gully, which was a bit of a joke, because that valley had never seen a real chimney.

* 1 foot is approximately 0.3 metres

85

The small bar in the river where Tatey first found gold was worked out on the second day, and we had to look elsewhere, but Tatey knew where to look, and as we had the river to ourselves we went upstream and found more gold. While I worked the cradle I kept watching the hills to see whether anyone else was coming into the valley. At first the hills seemed sinister, a threat to our security, but when no one came I began to grow tense, and wished someone would come and put an end to the waiting. I found the loneliness, after the crowd at Gabriels, hard to endure. I saw the sun come up and I saw it go down, and I saw the moon pass, but nothing else passed, unless you counted the wind, which often blew in the tussocks. It may sound strange, but I formed a kind of friendship with the stream, which was a river, really, low because of the fine autumn weather.

The river was always busy, and its voice was cheerful, as though it sang, and it was full of coloured stones, as well as gold. The stones were green or red or marble-white or speckled. The water was crystal-clear and no matter how often we muddied it, the mud would settle and the water run clear again.

86

The water was lovely to drink and made the best tea I have ever tasted. We washed in it, we ill-treated it, we stole from it, but it still ran clear and sang. Of course I said nothing of this to Tatey, who would have thought I was as mad as a hatter, and I didn't notice the river so much after Dan and Rex came.

Yes, they spotted us from the hill tops, and came scrambling down, and worked like beavers and they got so much gold their behaviour became rather peculiar, in that they became exaggeratedly secretive.

They set up camp near us, but no longer played cards with Tatey. They evidently thought there was more gold to be won from the river than to be won from Tatey, and, like us, they worked all the daylight hours, and slept like dead men at night. We were all on limited food supplies and knew that when the food we had brought with us was consumed we would have to return to the store at Gabriels for more, taking gold-dust with us to buy it, and that it would be very difficult to get back to Chimney Gully without being followed.

Ruth Dallas   Illustrated by Dick Evans

87

Flying high

Ring-billed gulls

Gulls following a trawler

Herring gulls

And there are times when we simply cannot run away from challenges which we have to face . . .

His first

The young seagull was alone on his ledge. His two brothers and his sister had already flown away the day before. He had been afraid to fly with them. Somehow when he had taken a little run forward to the brink of the ledge and attempted to flap his wings he became afraid. The great expanse of sea stretched down beneath, and it was such a long way down — miles* down. He felt certain that his wings would never support him, so he bent his head and ran away back to the little hole under the ledge where he slept at night. Even when each of his brothers and his little sister, whose wings were far shorter than his own, ran to the brink, flapped their wings, and flew away he failed to muster up courage to take that plunge which appeared to him so desperate. His father and mother had come around calling to him shrilly, upbraiding him, threatening to let him starve on his ledge unless he flew away. But for the life of him he could not move.

90

see pages 64–65

flight

That was twenty-four hours ago. Since then nobody had come near him. The day before, all day long, he had watched his parents flying about with his brothers and sister, perfecting them in the art of flight, teaching them how to skim the waves and how to dive for fish. He had, in fact, seen his older brother catch his first herring and devour it, standing on a rock, while his parents circled around raising a proud cackle. And all the morning the whole family had walked about on the big plateau midway down the opposite cliff, taunting him with his cowardice.

The sun was now ascending the sky, blazing warmly on his ledge that faced the north. He felt the heat because he had not eaten since the previous nightfall. Then he had found a dried piece of mackerel's tail at the far end of his ledge. Now there was not a single scrap of food left. He had searched every inch, rooting among the rough, dirt-caked straw nest where he and his brothers and sister had been hatched. He even gnawed at the dried pieces of spotted eggshell. It was like eating part of himself. He had then trotted back and forth from one end of the ledge to the other, his grey body the colour of the cliff, his long grey legs stepping daintily, trying to find some means of reaching his parents without having to fly.

ut on each side of him the ledge ended in a sheer fall of
precipice, with the sea beneath. And between him and
his parents there was a deep, wide chasm. Surely he
could reach them without flying if he could only move northwards
along the cliff face? But, then, on what could he walk? There was
no ledge, and he was not a fly. And above him he could see
nothing. The precipice was sheer, and the top of it was perhaps
farther away than the sea beneath him.

He stepped slowly out to the brink of the ledge, and, standing on
one leg, with the other leg hidden under his wing, he closed one
eye, then the other, and pretended to be falling asleep. Still they
took no notice of him. He saw his two brothers and his sister lying
on the plateau dozing, with their heads sunk into their necks. His
father was preening the feathers on his white back. Only his
mother was looking at him. She was standing on a little high hump
on the plateau, her white breast thrust forward. Now and again she
tore at a piece of fish that lay at her feet, and then scraped each
side of her beak on the rock. The sight of the food maddened him.
How he loved to tear food that way, scraping his beak now and
again to whet it! He uttered a low cackle. His mother cackled too,
and looked over at him.

"Ga, ga, ga," he cried, begging her to bring him over some food. "Gaw-ool-ah," she screamed back derisively. But he kept calling plaintively, and after a minute or so he uttered a joyful scream. His mother had picked up a piece of the fish and was flying across to him with it. He leaned out eagerly, tapping the rock with his feet, trying to get nearer to her as she flew across. But when she was just opposite to him, abreast of the ledge, she halted, her legs hanging limp, her wings motionless, the piece of fish in her beak almost within reach of his beak. He waited a moment in surprise, wondering why she did not come nearer, and then, maddened by hunger, he dived at the fish. With a loud scream he fell outwards and downwards into space. His mother had swooped upwards. As he passed beneath her he heard the swish of her wings. Then a monstrous terror seized him and his heart stood still. He could hear nothing. But it only lasted a moment. The next moment he felt his wings spread outwards. The wind rushed against his breast feathers, then under his stomach and against his wings. He could feel the tips of his wings cutting through the air. He was not falling headlong now. He was soaring gradually downwards and outwards.

He was no longer afraid. He just felt a bit dizzy. Then he flapped his wings once and he soared upwards. He uttered a joyous scream and flapped them again. He soared higher. He raised his breast and banked against the wind. "Ga, ga, ga. Ga, ga, ga. Gaw-ool-ah." His mother swooped past him, her wings making a loud noise. He answered her with another scream. Then his father flew over him screaming. Then he saw his two brothers and his sister flying around him, curving and banking and soaring and diving.

Then he completely forgot that he had not always been able to fly and he commenced to dive and soar and curvet, shrieking shrilly.

He was near the sea now, flying straight over it, facing straight out over the ocean. He saw a vast green sea beneath him, with little ridges moving over it, and he turned his beak sideways and crowed amusedly. His parents and his brothers and sister had landed on this green floor in front of him. They were beckoning to him, calling shrilly. He dropped his legs to stand on the green sea. His legs sank into it. He screamed with fright and attempted to rise again, flapping his wings. But he was tired and weak with hunger and he could not rise, exhausted by the strange exercise. His feet sank into the green sea, and then his belly touched it and he sank no farther. He was floating on it. And around him his family was screaming, praising him, and their beaks were offering him scraps of dog-fish.

He had made his first flight.

Liam O'Flaherty

Illustrated by Giovina Gaspari

94

words in flight

Glossary

abreast (*p. 93*)
side by side

acrid (*p. 72*)
bitter

arc (*p. 48*)
a curve

broke down (*p. 29*)
burst into tears

came to (*p. 47*)
to wake; regain
consciousness

careening (*p. 13*)
to dart from side to
side

compelled (*p. 72*)
forced

compulsion (*p. 66*)
strength; force

curvet (*p. 94*)
leap playfully

debris (*p. 48*)
the ruins; the
remains of
something that has
been destroyed

delicacies (*p. 8*)
things to eat that
are quite a luxury

Glossary continues on
page 96

disdained (*p. 72*)
disliked

disgruntled (*p. 23*)
annoyed and
disappointed

embers (*p. 42*)
glowing remains of
a fire

emigrates (*p. 37*)
to move to another
country

emphatically (*p. 67*)
forcefully

enticing (*p. 72*)
tempting

eye-glass (*p. 30*)
used to improve
eyesight in one eye
if it is not very
good

fervid (*p. 72*)
passionate

intensify (*p. 72*)
increase

loped (*p. 57*)
moved easily

mob-cap (*p. 34*)
a cap with a frill
round the edge

mouldering (*p. 72*)
crumbling

odourless (*p. 66*)
fresh; does not
smell

patented (*p. 58*)
if you have
invented
something, you
patent it so that
only you can sell or
make it

projecting (*p. 56*)
the piece of the
splint that is
sticking out

rack (*p. 70*)
make him
suffer; feel tired

racketing (*p. 4*)
making a noise

reflectors (*p. 52*)
small pieces of red
plastic or metal on
the back of a car
used to reflect the
headlights of
following traffic

remnant (*p. 55*)
the piece of stick
that's left

scarred-over (*p. 48*)
the fire had left
black burn marks

seared (*p. 68*)
burnt; scarred

skittered (*p. 8*)
ran quickly

snuffed (*p. 68*)
smelled

splint (*p.47*)
a support for
broken bones

still (*p. 39*)
a photograph
taken from a scene
in a film

thicket (*p. 66*)
where trees grow
closely

waterhole (*p. 42*)
a natural hole or
hollow containing
water